I0570665

RANDOM WALK IN MY LIBRARY

Jorge Pinto Mazal

Jorge Pinto Books Inc.

```
JORGE
PINTO
BOOKS
```

Random Walk in My Library

Copyright © 2017 by Jorge Pinto Mazal

All rights reserved. This book may not be reproduced in whole or in part, in any form (beyond copying permitted by Sections 107 and 108 of the United States Copyright Law, and except limited excerpts by reviewer for the public press), without written permission from Jorge Pinto Books Inc. 6216 Vorlich Lane, Bethesda, Md. 20816

Book design by Old and the New ONEW

ISBN 978-1-934978-90-0

1-934978-90-6

To Tania, Flavia and Natalia for their inspiring personalities,
as well as to their beautiful families.

To Christine Tsui hua for her suggestions and patience
to read these reviews.

To Pepe for his useful advise and Sylvia for being close.

With special thanks to my friend and author Marta
Merajver-Kulat for her time editing the texts.

INDEX

Random Walk in my Library

Introduction

The title *Random Walk by my Library* is prompted by what I regularly do; walk by my library, look at the covers and pull out different books that I read in the past and want to browse or, in some cases, read again. The series of reviews included in this book is the result of these walks. Apparently, there is no particular reason for the choice, but now that they are together I can see some patterns and some underlying themes that attracted my attention and desire to share my views on these texts.

Some of these reviews have connections. Several have a relation to everyday human tragedies, mostly examples of deceit, seduction, adultery, and their consequences. *Anna Karenina* by Leon Tolstoy, *Adolphe* by Benjamin Constant, *The Left Handed Woman* by Peter Handke fit this description. In the first two titles, the main characters deceive and mistreat women. In Peter Handke's book, men, for short term satisfaction, to bust their ego or just for fun try to take advantage of a lonely, recently divorced woman. Without a clear connection with seduction, I think Sándor Márai's *Portraits of a Marriage* gives an excellent panorama of the conflicting relationships between women and men.

Terrorism is another topic found in books with fanatics as the main characters or individuals manipulated by governments that use terror to promote their interests. Here I reviewed two Joseph

Conrad masterpieces: *Under the Western Eyes* and *The Secret Agent*, both written over a hundred years ago. Unfortunately, the issues brilliantly described in the plots of these two novels are still present in our days with bloodier results, religious fanaticism and better organized terrorist organizations.

Another set of books is a selection of letters written by famous people like those between Thomas Mann and Hermann Hesse, two great Nobel Prize Winners. Also, in this category are the letters by Vincent van Gogh, Franz Kafka, and Sigmund Freud. I can add the classic book of Rainer Maria Rilke: *Letters to a Young Poet*, addressed to one of his admirers, Franz Xaver Kappus, a 19-year-old cadet who preserved the letters that have attracted many young poets and writers.

Other reviews are difficult to categorize. They include classics that are ideal companions to understand the complexity of our human nature. I chose for these reasons Albert Camus' *The Fall*; Mario Vargas Llosa's *The Notebooks of Don Rigoberto*; Irvin D. Yalom's *When Nietzsche Wept*; Walker Percy's *Lancelot* and *On Reading* by Marcel Proust.

Finally, I added a review of a non-fiction book, *The War that ended Peace* by Margaret McMillan, commemorating the 100th anniversary of World War I, which killed millions, devastated Europe and was the prelude to a second, more deadly war a few years later.

As a fictional context to describe the horrors of war in families, friends, and individuals, I included a brief review of *The Radetzky* March by Joseph Roth.

Ever since ancient times, libraries have become the custodians of knowledge and human wisdom. Many are admired for their design and mostly by their assets and content. Their primary purpose is to collect, organize, store and preserve all kinds of books, reading materials, movies, music and, in today's world, all sorts of digital content.

One of the most important libraries is Babel, a biblical myth of a tower that represents a world without language barriers. It will grow so high that it will eventually reach heaven. Based on that idea, paintings by famous artists depict it in different fashions. One of the most famous was painted by Bruegel the Elder.

The mythical library has also inspired fiction writers, mainly Jorge Luis Borges. In his short story, *The Library of Babel*, he writes, "The universe (which others call the Library) is composed of an indefinite, perhaps infinite number of hexagonal galleries." Borges playfully mentions some of the books in the library that created serious conflicts among their inhabitants. Borges's story speaks about the influences exerted by books, telling us that "it was assured, there must exist a book that is the cipher and perfect compendium of 'all other books', and some librarian must have examined that book; this librarian is analogous to a god. In the language of this zone there are still vestiges of the sect that worshiped that distant librarian. "/1

The library of Alexandria is another vital reference, not mythical like Babel, but solidly built in the 3d Century BC. and conceived as a research center that hosted manuscripts and rolls from all over the world and the most varied cultures. Unfortunately, the Library was burned several times, including the occasion when Julius Caesar's army conquered Egypt. The destruction of this historic institution represents a significant cultural loss and an irreparable damage to human knowledge.

There are hundreds of famous libraries created during centuries around the world. Running the risk of leaving out many important and relevant institutions randomly, I have selected a few for their beautiful well-stocked collections, listed in an Annex at the end of the book.

There are also many libraries from famous writers, businesspeople, and politicians. Some of these are open to the public.

Walter Benjamin, the famous writer and media philosopher, dedicated several essays to his library and other writers' libraries. He also explored the issues faced by book collectors like him, particularly the joy of buying rare books and the frustration of being outbid by wealthier collectors in auctions. In one of Benjamin's famous essays, *Unpacking My Library, a Talk about Book Collecting,*/2 he gives an insight into "the relationship of a book collector to his possessions," or "collecting rather than a collection."

In another paragraph that turned out tragically prophetic on his fate a few years later when he was escaping the Nazis, depressed at losing his precious library, he says, "You have all heard of people whom the loss of their books has turned into invalids, or of those who to acquire them became criminals." Benjamin sadly experienced that ordeal as a refugee forced to abandon his collection and took his own life on the border between Spain and France.

Libraries have many puzzling stories, some fictional, some real. Umberto Eco, *The Name of the Rose*, is one example. A more recent one is found in Irvin D. Yalom's novel *The Spinoza Problem*. In the introduction, he gives a powerful example of the importance of books owned by the famous philosopher Baruch Spinoza. Yalom describes a visit he paid to the philosopher's museum in Rijnsburg, Holland. There, looking at Spinoza's 150 volume collection, he got the inspiration he was seeking to write the novel, third in a series based on famous philosophers: Nietzsche, Schopenhauer, and Spinoza. Yalom was told by the museum guide that after the invasion of Holland, the "ERR 'Einsatzstab Reichsleiter Rosenberg', the taskforce of Reich leader Rosenberg...the major Nazi anti-Semitic ideologue troops... stole everything—the books, a bust, and a portrait of Spinoza—everything. They carted it all away, then sealed and expropriated the museum."

Yalom was surprised to hear that the books were miraculously returned intact to the museum after the war in 1946. He wondered why something so modest was in the looting agenda of the Nazi leader. The guide continues giving Yalom more puzzling information: "they had some mysterious interest in Spinoza. In his official report, Rosenberg's officer, the Nazi who did the hands-on looting of the library, added a significant sentence: 'They contain valuable early works of great importance for the exploration of the Spinoza problem." As in his last novels, Yalom used these facts to work on a plot, paying particular attention to why these books were preserved rather than burnt as thousands of others torched by the Nazis and on 'the Spinoza problem,' a phrase he uses as the title of his novel.

Libraries are also common themes for visual artist. One example is the work of a young Mexican artist, Emilio Chapela, who designed wooden objects and spaces that enrich the debate about the future of libraries and books by leaning into a renewed category of books – the book as an object in an art form./3

Another very moving example is the installation produced by the Iraqi artist Wafaa Bilal, titled *168:01*, of an austere white library with a series of white shelves filled with blank tomes. This work is conceived as a monument to the staggering cultural losses endured throughout the history of Iraq, including the loss of 70,000 volumes burnt during the 2002 war. The work "doubles as a system of exchange connecting its physical and virtual visitors to the College of Fine Arts in Iraq."

Organizing a collection has its rules, which mainly apply to public libraries. Personal libraries, in contrast, allow their owners to be capricious and use highly private classification methods. People organize their libraries in very different forms; alphabetic by author or title, and also by themes and genre: in fiction, mystery, romance, poetry; in nonfiction, biographies, travel, business, politics, illustrated, photography, etc. Collectors that like symmetry put together books of the same size or colors, naturally making it challenging to find a particular title.

Alberto Mangel, a renowned historian of libraries and books, in his *The Library at Night* describes one of the methods used in ancient China and known as the largest encyclopedia ever printed. He tells us how each section "..covers one specific realm of human concern, such as Science or Travel, and is divided into subsections containing biographical entries." Mangel continues, "The section on Human Relations, for instance, lists the biographies of thousands of men and women according to their occupation or position in society, among them sages, slaves, playboys, tyrants, doctors, calligraphers, supernatural beings, great drinkers, notable archers and widows who did not marry again."/4

I don't have a method since, as the title of this book suggests, my libraries are randomly organized. I sometimes put together books by the same author and, in other shelves, books written in the same language. In principle, I separate fiction from nonfiction books, keeping a very imprecise memory map to know where a title is located to find it when I need it. In any case, I have to walk along the bookshelves, trying to identify what I am searching for.

Having grown in a home with a relatively extensive library mostly composed of literature books, I started reading at a very early age. My father was a Medical Doctor, therefore, we also had anatomy books and medical manuals. I don't recall it as having a particular order, but remember some titles like *The Magic Mountain* by Thomas Mann, *The Second Sex* by Simone De Beauvoir, *My Sister, My Spouse: A Biography of Lou Andreas-Salomé* by H.F. Peters, Agatha Christie's *Murder in the Orient Express*, Sor Juana Ines de la Cruz's *Los Empeños de una Casa*; *The Outsider* by Camus, *La Region mas Transparente* by Carlos Fuentes, Juán Rulfo's *Pedro Páramo* and *Casi El Paraiso* by Luis Spota, and many more.

I started collecting books in high school besides the academic required texts and enjoyed going to 'Librería Cristal', a bookstore near home, in Mexico City. I spent time browsing the display tables. After finishing college, I was lucky to be in charge of the book review section of a political magazine for almost two years. Publishers and authors sent me dozens of fiction and nonfiction books every month. Soon I was able to have an excellent library with its shelves filling quickly and needed to build extra bookcases on the wall of my home staircase.

My love of books grew even stronger when I had the opportunity to become an editor selecting one relevant chapter from classic political books to form a collection of small and cheap booklets no more than 50 pages long. The collection was *Cuadernos de Divulgación Política Clásica* (notebooks to disseminate political classics). The idea was to attract new readers and facilitate the discovery of essential works that, written centuries ago, continue to inform the present.

A few years ago, I became a book publisher. I aimed to promote a culture of reading to understand today's human problems. With this goal in mind, I asked Marta Merajver-Kurlat, an Argentinean novelist, translator, essayist, and biographer to write a series of books for a collection titled "Bibliotreatment." Among the four titles is *Reading for Personal Development*,/4 whose central idea is that reading is therapeutic.

There are dozens if not thousands of lists of titles anyone should read. Many writers have published or mentioned in interviews which are their favorite books. By way of example, I think of Leo Tolstoy's List of the *50+ Books That Influenced Him Most* (1891)./5 In an article published in Esquire in 1935, Hemingway listed seventeen books that were among his favorites/6. Henry Miller wrote *The Books in My Life* including a list of one hundred titles that had influenced him./7

Also, every year newspapers publish their list of the best 50 or 100 best books of the year.

There are different kinds of readers, depending on their circumstance. People debate what type of book one should take to a desert island. A more serious issue related to this topic is deciding what books to read for specific situations. We always wonder which books to take when traveling by airplane or boat or any other means of transport and what to read in waiting rooms, etc. There are countless situations and tastes and ultimately, what to read is a subjective decision.

I am working on reviews of books by women writers. I have already randomly selected from my library books that had a profound impact on my life and that, just as the books in this volume, are also essential classics. I hope soon to have a second volume with the reviews of *Lou Adreas Salome' Letters to Rilke*, Jane Austen's, Charlotte's and Emily Brontë's novels, Simone de Beauvoir's *The Second Sex*, Iris Murdoch's *The Sea the Sea*, Carson McCullers's *The Ballad of the Sad Cafe*; Virginia Wolf's *A Room of One's Own* and Anais Nin's *In Favor of the Sensitive Man*.

I sincerely hope the reviews that follow will invite readers to take a plunge and read the full books. I am sure they will be rewarded.

NOTES:

1) Jorge Luis Borges, *The Library of Babel*. Collected Fictions. Trans. Andrew Hurley. NewYork: Penguin, 1998.

2) Benjamin, Walter, *1892–1940.Illuminations.*Translation of: Illuminationen.Reprint. Originally published: New York: Harcourt, Brace & World, 1968. Excerpt From: Walter Benjamin. "Illuminations." iBooks. https://itunes.apple.com/us/book/illuminations/id535866529?mt=11

3) Emilio Chapela. *Die Kurt F. Gödel Bibliothek: A Book about Books*. Sicomoro Ediciones, 2015

4) Alberto Mangel. *Library at Night*. Yale University Press. 2006

5) Marta Merajver-Kurlat. *Reading for Personal Development*, Jorge Pinto Books Inc. 2011.

6) Leo Tolstoy. *List of the 50+ Books That Influenced Him Most* (1891).
http://www.openculture.com/2014/07/leo-tolstoy-creates-a-list-of-the-50-books-that-influenced-him-most-1891.html

7) Ernest Hemingway. *Remembering Shooting-Flying: A Key West Letter*. Esquire magazine, 1935

8). Henry Miller. *The Books in my Life*, New Directions Publishing Corporation (1969)

Benjamin Constant's *Adolphe* and

the Power of Destructive Love

Adolphe is a sorrowful classic novella by Benjamin Constant, first published in London and Paris in 1816. The book has captivated numerous scholars and romantic readers who are lucky to discover it. In 2002 french director Benoît Jacquot adapted Adolphe into a film starring the celebrated actress Isabelle Adjani.

Benjamin Constant was born in Lausanne Switzerland and is best known for his books on politics. He was an active liberal political figure at the end of the French Revolution as a member of the Directory in 1799 and then of the "Tribunal", but was forced to resign by Napoleon Bonaparte for his radical ideas on democratic rules as well as usurpation of power which form the core of his writings.

Some believes that *Adolphe* is an autobiographical novella since Constant happened to be a seducer as well in his real life. Like Adolphe, he also pursued older women or neglected wives who tend to be vulnerable emotional-wise, making them easy preys of skilful lovers.

Constant had a 15-year long romantic relation with Germaine de Staël, with whom he became very close politically and emotionally. She was forced to exile from Napoleon's Paris and settled in Château de Coppet near Geneva where she organised famous gatherings of "Salon" style, attended by refugees and political thinkers to talk about international events. Before *Adophe* was published, Mme de Staël had written two novels which can be seen as "inversed mirror" of Constant's novella since the victim is not a tormented married woman who becomes madly in love with a younger and selfish lover as in *Adolph*, but a married man that falls in love with a woman who makes him suffer as she does with other men. Like Constant, Mme de Staël also used the main characters' names as the titles of novels – *Corinne* (1802) and *Delphine* (1807).

There has been three editions of *Adolphe*, in 1816, 1824 and 1828 respectively. Each of the second and third came with a preface explaining why the work was reprinted. The novella exists in the form of a diary of a young man which is sent by the inn keeper in a box to a publisher who is stranded by a snow storm and comes across a stranger who happens to be the writer and who has vanished. The content of the mysterious box is described by the publisher as "a quantity of very old letters either unaddressed or on which the addresses and as signatures were illegible, a woman's portrait and a notebook containing the anecdote or story you are about to read." The fictional publisher remembers that stranger as "..very silent and looked sad. He showed no impatience. Now and again, as he was the only man in the place to whom I could talk" and "when the roads were reopened and we could have set off, the stranger fell seriously ill".

Adolphe, the narrator of the novella recalls that at the age of twenty two his father, a government official, sent him "on a tour of the most interesting European countries" where he leads "a very dissipated life". He looks back to the moment when he falls in love with Ellénore, a married woman who is ten years older than him. Initially she turns down this younger suitor who uses his charms to win over her love. She eventually gives up her stable and privileged status and abandons her husband for a short, passionate and then, in the end, painful love affair.

In the beginning Adolphe finds profound pleasure with his seducing adventure and describes how "younger men.. were delighted with the skill with which I had supplanted the Count", i.e. Ellénore's husband, and "congratulated me on my conquest and undertook to imitate me."

However, Ellénore feels the opposite as she "soon realised that opinion was turning against her". Women friends including family members, "broke off the connexion with the greatest possible ostentation". Men, on the other hand, "came …because she was still a attractive and her recent frailty had given them aspirations they made no effort to disguise."

The happy beginning of the affair soon brings disgrace and social isolation. Adolphe's father who cares about his son's future career decides to break the relationship. At the same time Adolphe is getting bored and trying to end an affair which becomes a heavy emotional as well as social burden. The book focuses on the feelings and state of mind of a desperate lover, that is Ellénore, who suffers to see her beloved becoming distant which almost reaches a point of cruelty.

Adolph is aware that Ellénore has sacrificed everything for him, now that she is socially cut-off and continues to be attached and deeply in love with him. He also perceives that a separation will bring utter despair and pain to her which might lead to a suicide.

There are many stories about enduring love which is made possible only when each of the couple is "lover" and "beloved" at the same time. Somehow it is not the case with Adolphe, which deals with unhealthy relationships pursued by immature egocentric seducers who target fragile persons, which always have tragic endings since the seducers, once achieve their conquests, stop being a pursuing "lover" but, for vanity's sake, allow themselves to be "loved" and thus cause enormous pain.

There are many other novels which follow the same pattern, such as Senso, written by Camillo Boito and adapted into film by Luccino Visconti in 1954. *The Ballad of the Sad Cafe* by Carlson MaCullers brilliantly portrays this type of relationship. When she describes a love relationship, she distinguishes the "lover" and the "beloved". Clearly "the beloved is only a stimulus for all the stored-up love which has lain quiet within the lover for a long time... The beloved may be treacherous, greasy-headed, and given to evil habits. Yes, and the lover may see this as clearly as anyone else—but that does not affect the evolution of his love one whit." – this is how the prototype of the character Adolphe could be depicted by the author of the Ballad.

Benjamin Constant In this brief novella explores with considerable knowledge the social context in the post French Revolution Europe and shows a profound understanding of individual feelings and the psychological state of mind of those who confuse love with infatuation.

Excerpts From:
Benjamin Constant. *Adolphe.*. Penguin Books, 1964 iBooks.

https://itunes.apple.com/us/book/adolphe/id374925591?
mt=11

Carson McCullers *The Ballad of the Sad Cafe.* Houghton
Mifflin Harcourt Cafe. 2005.

https://itunes.apple.com/us/book/the-ballad-of-the-sad-cafe/
id429702512?mt=11

Benjamin Constant. *The Spirit of Conquest and Usurpation*,
in *Political Writings*, trans. and ed. by Biancamaria Fontana
(Cambridge, Eng.: Cambridge University Press, 1988)

Anna Karenina: Tolstoy's obsessive eye on love, jealousy, adultery and the decline of Russian aristocracy.

War and Peace and *Anna Karenina* are the two greatest works by Tolstoy, the former published in 1869, the latter published in installments from 1873 to 1877. They are regularly compared in terms of the difference in style. For some scholars, the inclusion of essays in a narrative that tends to be fictitious makes it difficult to categorize *War and Peace* as a novel. Tolstoy wrote an interpretative note entitled A Few Words on *War and Peace* in which he explicitly confirmed that this work "is not a novel, even less is it a poem, and still less a historical chronicle." This explanation by the author makes *Anna Karenina* his first novel. Another important difference is the time where the two works take place. *War and Peace* happens during the French invasion of Russia in 1812 whereas *Anna Karenina* in the years when it was written. As a serial, it took several years to be completed, allowing Tolstoy to witness and describe through his characters, how the society was changing, including his ideas about his country and his own class.

Considered as one of Tolstoy's masterpieces, *Anna Karenina* is best known for its outstanding portraits of the compelling characters and extraordinary situations in the story. It has the typical Tolstoy's signature style to allow the readers to explore the complex personalities of the characters, and to learn about their most intimate desires and emotions as well as ideas and tastes. The novel is full of interesting dialogues and conversations among various topics, ranging from the most frivolous gossips to highly sophisticated issues such as education, religion, morality, and politics, etc.

One of Tolstoy talents is to create distinct, believable characters that the readers quickly identify with, describing in detail their actions, ideas, and intimate thoughts. Tolstoy's writing is an invitation for the readers to be the witnesses by sharing the atmosphere of different situations like attending events such as a ball, a concert, a dinner, a hunting trip or a horse race. His rich language helps us discover where his ideological affinities and antipathies lie in respectively. Many times his characters impersonate a part of himself or are inspired by close friends or family members which makes his novels somewhat autobiographical especially when he makes Konstantin Levin, one the story leading characters, a kindred soul.

The novel also highlights the situations of the arrogant declining aristocracy challenged by only a few progressive reformers as well as the rising 'nouveau-riche' that embraces the luxuries and a colorful lifestyle. Some from the old world aristocracy are struggling to keep up their expensive level of living with increased debt and a rapidly diminished inheritance or income from the land.

There is also another type of aristocrats that can be contented with a simple life. They are truly concerned about the problems confronting the peasants and think that land is a relatively important issue in Russia compared to the rest of

Europe.

Tolstoy also shows the double-standard morality of the Moscow and Petersburg high society that ostracizes the heroine Anna, who chooses to sacrifice her honor and her family for the sake of love.

After finishing the last chapters of *Anna Karenina* Tolstoy renegaded his aristocratic background and concentrated on "morally improving tales". He published dozens of pamphlets and essays promoting anti-establishment Christian values in an attempt to foment social change. Two years after Anna Karenina was released in 1889 Tolstoy finished The Kreutzer Sonata, initially banned, a novella that was considered to be one of the best books on jealousy and sexual obsession. Many critics think that it matches William Shakespeare's *Othello*, Fyodor Dostoevsky's *The Eternal Husband*, Thomas Hardy's *Tess of the D'Urbervilles*, and many other great novels or plays dealing with these complex dark emotional attributes of destructive human relationships.

In Anna Karenina, unfaithfulness or adultery is one of the central topics entangled with jealousy that also troubles many other characters in the novel.

It is possible to find some similarities between *Anna Karenina* and other 19th Century romantic novels where certain heroines are married to an older man with high positions in society and break their marriages fatally falling in love with young officials. As an avid reader of French literature and politics, Tolstoy was familiar and probably read *Adolph*, the classic novella by Benjamin Constant. In both stories, the heroine fall in love with young and attractive official, Anna with Vronsky and Ellénore with Adolph. Both give up their stable and privileged status and abandon their husbands. They lose a comfortable life and are rejected by the society. However, the similarities end there since the stories unfold in a different way.

Anna is not abandoned by her suitor whereas Ellénore is. Even though proud of his conquest, Vronsky is captivated by Anna's looks and personality and ardently pursues her, regardless of the consequences of getting involved with a married woman. He makes no excuses and wants to live together with Anna and even proposes marriage. Adolph, on the other hand, brags about his conquest and indulges himself thinking that "younger men.. were delighted with the skill with which I had supplanted the Count (i. e. Ellénore's husband)," They, congratulated me on my conquest and undertook to imitate me." For Ellénore, it is a short, passionate love affair, that in the end, brings great pain.

Vronsky is madly in love with Anna and faces the challenges. He openly evaluates the available options. Reflecting their situation he quietly thinks; "If I told her to leave her husband, that must mean uniting her life with mine; am I prepared for that? How can I take her away now, when I have no money? Supposing I could arrange.... But how can I take her away while I'm in the service? If I say that—I ought to be prepared to do it, that is, I ought to have the money and to retire from the army." Money should not necessarily be a problem, since his family is immensely wealthy to allow them a comfortable life abroad. He is even ready to sacrifice a promising military career for Anna in Russia.

Vronsky also knows that his decision has very minor social

risks and could even enhance his image as a sophisticated, worldly man. "He was very well aware that he ran no risk of being ridiculous in the eyes of .. fashionable people. He was very well mindful of the fact that in their eyes .. the position of a man pursuing a married woman, and, regardless of everything, staking his life on drawing her into adultery, has something elegant and grand about it, and can never be ridiculous;....."

However, the impact is somewhat different on Anna's side. She needs to make the greatest sacrifice of leaving her loved child. And, opposite to the admiration that Anna's suitor draws from certain social circles, she is made an outcast by most of her "friends," who turn their back and harshly criticize her. Tolstoy's description of the rough responses to Anna's conduct shows one of the darkest sides of the Russian aristocracy. "The greater number of the young women, who envied Anna and had long been weary of hearing her called virtuous, rejoiced at the fulfillment of their predictions, and were only waiting for a decisive turn in public opinion to fall upon her with all the weight of their scorn. They were already making ready their handfuls of mud to fling at her when the right moment arrived. The greater number of the middle-aged people and certain great personages were displeased at the prospect of the impending scandal in society."

Anna and Vronsky are not the only important characters in the novel. Anna's brother Stepan Arkadyich Oblonsky (Stiva) and his friend Konstantin Levin, who later becomes his brother-in-law, also have great significances. They embodies two very different personalities exhibiting the contrast between the two styles in the old aristocracy in Russia at the time.

Oblonsky is a well regarded government official but at the same time becomes very irresponsible with his financial situation continuing to borrow money to maintain a high living standard. While he indulges himself with fancy dinners, his family are struggling and have to endure the inconveniences with their summer country house which is in dire need of visible repairs. On top of this, he is also an unfaithful husband and caused social humiliation on his family.

As a contrast, Levin is a character that represents Tolstoy values and ideas. He enjoys a straightforward austere life in the country coexisting with the peasants. Being a member of the aristocracy that owns land, he decides to stay far from what he considers a frivolous city life. Levin is also intellectually engaged, writing a book on agriculture with the particular problems the peasants and land owners face in Russia. He is an idealist that dreams of a non-violent revolution among the following lines. "This is not a matter of myself individually; the question of the public welfare comes into it. The whole system of culture, the chief element in the condition of the people, must be completely transformed. Instead of poverty, general prosperity, and content; instead of hostility, harmony and unity of interests. In short, a bloodless revolution, but a revolution of the greatest magnitude, beginning in the little circle of our district, then the province, then Russia, the whole world."

The clash of personalities between the two characters is described in different chapters of the novel, particularly when Arkadyevitch, facing bankruptcy, decided to sell a forest without consulting his friend Levin, who knows the buyer and the price of the land is baffled when Oblonsky mention the terms of the operation "'Then you've as good as given away your forest for nothing,' said Levin gloomily." Surprised Stepan Arkadyevitch reply, "How do you mean for nothing?" with a good-humored smile" and with distinct arrogant tone explicitly referring to Levin continue "Oh, these farmers!" said Stepan Arkadyevitch playfully. "Your tone of contempt for us poor townsfolk!... But when it comes to business, we do it better than anyone. I assure you I have reckoned it all out," he said, "and the forest is fetching a very good price.."

Tolstoy also includes a minor character to mock the "nouveau-riche" aristocracy. The author introduces the pompous Vasenka Veslovsky who is invited by Arkadyevitch to visit Levin in the country, "a brilliant young gentleman in Petersburg and Moscow society. "A capital fellow, and a keen sportsman," Stepan Arkadyevitch said, introducing him." Levin has a different impression seeing his unexpected guest as "a quite uncongenial and superfluous person."

Tolstoy makes a caricature of this "gentleman" when the three go hunting the next day. Pretending to be at home in the country, he uses a different outfit, appearing in a pair of expensive new boots and an exotic hat. "Vassenka Veslovsky had had no notion before that it was truly chic for a sportsman to be in tatters, but to have his shooting outfit of the best quality. He saw it now as he looked at Stepan Arkadyevitch, radiant in his rags, graceful, well-fed, and joyous, a typical Russian nobleman. And he made up his mind that next time he went shooting he would certainly adopt the same get-up."

It is not the intention of this long note to go through the vivid descriptions of all the characters and situations encompassed in this novel. Many critical characters are not included here as are the cases of Anna's husband whose anger and dilemmas facing his wife's affair, and Kitty, Levin's wife, who deals with his jealousy when newly wedded. I also did not include here Tolstoy's brilliant accounts of an election, the discussion of the music played in a concert, the interesting conversations over some sumptuous dinners, and much more.

The idea of this review, like the others, is to encourage those readers that have not yet had the opportunity to try this masterpiece and those who, like me, read it a long time ago, to look for it in their library or to download a copy, even for free, with their iPad to enjoy it again.

Anna Karenina is a work of art that allow the readers to enjoy and learn from Tolstoy's incisive psychological skills about the universal human conditions, independently of time and place. As a masterpiece classic, this title will be permanently available in print and eBook or any other up-to-date formats for the enjoyment of future generations.

Excerpts from:

Leon Tolstoi. *Anna Karenina*. Penguin Classics. 2001

The Left Handed Woman by Peter Handke. On Women's Freedom from the Bondage of Undesirable Marriage

The Left-Handed Woman is probably one of Peter Handke's best known novellas, translated into more than a dozen of languages. Two years after being published in 1978, it was made into a film that Handke adapted and directed. The film was nominated for the "Golden Palm Award" at the Cannes Film Festival and has won several prestigious prizes.

Handke was born in Carinthia, Austria in 1942. In his early years he endured painful experiences from the horrors of Nazism and World War II. A Sorrow Beyond Dreams, a poignant memoir was probably inspired by some ordeals from his childhood – a broken family with a drunken stepfather and a mother who committed suicide. His works tend to incorporate several aspects of the complex relationship between parents and children, a subject that is also present in *The Left-Handed Woman*. At the beginning of Handke's co-written multi-award winning film Wings of Desire (co-authored with its director Wim Wenders), a homesick voice dealing with a child from Song of Childhood, his most famous poem, was used. Below I am quoting a few lines to offer you a taste of the nostalgic tone.

> "When the child was a child
> It walked with its arms swinging,
> wanted the brook to be a river,
> the river to be a torrent,

and this puddle to be the sea."

As a multi-talented artist and one of the most recognized living German-language writers, Handke has produced dozens of books including poetry, novel, essay, memoir, translation and controversial theatre plays that he directed and acted. He was also quite active in films, writing many screenplays, particularly the adaptations of his own novels Absence and *The Left-Handed Woman* which he directed, as well as *City of Angels* directed by Bradley Siberling and *Wings of Desire* directed by Wim Wenders as mentioned earlier.

Marianne, the main character in The Left-Handed Woman, is 30 years old and most of the time in the story she is only referred as "the Woman". She is married to Bruno, who is constantly travelling as the "sales manager of the local branch of a porcelain concern well known throughout Europe". They have one child, Stephan, a quiet and detached boy who is referred to sometimes in the novella as "the child". They "lived in a terraced bungalow colony on the south slope of a low mountain range in western Germany, just above the fumes of a big city."

Other relevant characters in the novella are Franziska, a close friend of the couple and the teacher of the child. Like the main character, some of the characters are also named by only a generic name to refer to their identity or profession. The Publisher is a former boss of the woman, who is "a heavyset but rather fidgety man of fifty" who dates younger women. The Father of the Woman, another character, brings into the story the Actor when he identifies him in the street and brazenly tells him that he was "not shameless enough for an actor. You want to be a personality, like the actors in those

American movies, but you never risk yourself. As a result, you're always posing." Two additional characters with minor roles are the Chauffeur of the Publisher and the Salesgirl, a single mother with a baby.

Handke uses a family as a microcosm to display the problems of many women in Europe, especially in Germany who suffer from dependency on domineering husbands. They live isolated in suburbs taking care of children that are often absent-minded or spoiled, and not quite close or loving.

From the beginning of the novella one can easily spot Bruno as a selfish man that treats his wife as a docile object to fulfill his selfish needs. Handke manages to disclose this authoritarian nature when Marianne pick ups Bruno from the airport after he has been traveling for weeks. Bruno talks to her in a bossy tone and doesn't seem to care for her opinions, "Let's go to the hotel in town for a festive dinner. It's too private here for my taste right now. Too—haunted. I would like you to wear your low-cut dress." Without objecting to this command, Marianne asks him "What will you wear?" .... "Bruno: "I'll go just as I am." The same thing happens again at the end of the dinner, when Bruno tells her, "We'll spend the night here. Stefan knows where we are. I left the telephone number on his bedside table." The woman lowers her eyes while Bruno tells the waiter. "I need a room for the night," he said. "You see, my wife and I want to sleep together right away."

In this sequence early in the story, Handke makes explicit the desire of Marianne's to move away from an inconsiderate husband and to live alone with their son. Walking back home the morning after the night at the hotel, Marianne tells Bruno without warning: "I suddenly had an illumination...that you were going away, that you were leaving me. Yes, that's it. Go away, Bruno. Leave me."

From that moment, the story starts to focus on the Woman's new life without a husband, including the struggle with loneliness and the need to adapt to a situation that she has created without regrets. The story unravels through descriptions of her daily routine, her relationship with the child and her encounters with the other characters.

One day the Woman comes across her friend Franziska who asks her "Is there someone else?" She also shows concern for the well-being of her and the child's, "What will the two of you live on? Have you thought of that?" But at the same time, Franziska is impressed by Marianne's action and invites her to join her in a women's group meeting. "They'll all be so glad to have you. Right now they have a feeling that human thought is in pretty good shape but that life is elsewhere. We need someone who's making a bit of a break with the normal way of life—in other words, who's slightly nuts."

One evening, the Publisher appears at Marianne's door without previous notice to respond to her, as she has sent him a letter to let him know that she is now in a position to accept his offers to translate for him as in the past. He enters with "flowers in one hand and a bottle of champagne in the other" and says, "I knew you were alone, Marianne." With this scene, Handke seems to imply that the Publisher expects more than translation work and desires to have a "romantic" night with his new employee. Like many men, he thought divorced or separated women were in need of company, therefore, easy to seduce.

The Actor also appears at Marianne's door another day approaching her in a more subtle way with romantic "poetic" words, expressing his desire to have a relationship with her: "There are some galaxies so distant that their light is weaker than the mere background glow of the night sky. I would like to be somewhere else with you now." Insistent on her decision to be alone and probably assuming that these sweet words at the end will turn out to be empty and worthless, the Woman answers, "Please don't put me in any of your plans."

With these two events involving Marianne's intending lovers, Handke seems to show a certain disdain for men that try to grasp weaker women to fulfill their selfish needs either of sex or of ego. Handke further challenges all stereotypes involving this context in his modern attempt on the classic figure *Don Juan: His Own Version* (published in English in 2011). Handke's Don Juan travels through different countries and gets in bed with many women, yet he is not a simple seducer. "His power over women is of a different order, and he does not revel in it; on the contrary, it makes him shy. His look ... reveals to them the "outrage" of their solitude and sets free their desire, which he then feels duty-bound to fulfil".

However, in *The Left-Handed Woman*, male characters are different from Handke's "Don Juan". Marianne is not necessarily a feminist nor does she dislike men, but prefers to keep them at a distance. Clearly she chooses solitude rather than having another authoritarian boyfriend like her husband or a fling with an idealist romantic man who might flicker and fade. Marianne, "..looked into her eyes and said, 'You haven't given yourself away. And no one will ever humiliate you again.'"

The title The Left-handed Woman is taken from a song to which Marianne listens alone "over and over again". The lyrics make reference to a woman like Marianne, who sits "with others in a Laudromat,"; comes "out of with others from the metro exit" or "from an office building". The tune continues as if mirroring Marianne's isolated daily life: "She sat with others on the edge of a playground, But once I saw her through a window Playing chess all alone". The song ends telling the left-handed woman: "I want to see you in a foreign continent, For there at last I shall see you alone among others, And among a thousand others you will see me, And at last we shall go to meet each other."

———————

Excerpts from:

Peter Handke. *Left Handed Women*. iBooks. https://itun.es/us/WcdGD.l

Originally published in German under the title Die linkshändige Frau, ©1976 by Suhrkamp Verlag, Frankfurt am Main". English translation "Published simultaneously in the USA and Canada in 1997 by McGraw-Hill Ryerson Ltd., Toronto"

Joel Agee. *Man of Constant Sorrow*, New York Times, February 12, 2010. Link: http://www.nytimes.com/2010/02/14/books/review/Agee-t.html?scp=1&sq=joel%20agee&st=cse&_r=0

Peter Handke. *Don Juan: His Own Version*, Translated by Krishna Winston, Farrar, Straus & Giroux, 2011.

Sándor Márai's *Portraits of a Marriage* and its First Person Perspective

Like Albert Camus in his novella The Fall, Sándor Márai, a great contemporary Hungarian writer, also uses "First Person" perspective in his novel *Portraits of a Marriage*.

It is divided in three parts, for each of the three characters, where each's intimate past in connection with the other two is unveiled.

Ilona, a divorcee, Peter her ex husband and Judit the reason for whom the marriage between the two eventually comes to an end.

The book is written in a powerful and engaging language that makes a reader feel involved as an intruding listener of a private conversation that the character has with a companion or a confidant. Each has a distinct perspective of his/her past and the conflicting background of his/her relationships with the other two.

The book opens with Ilonka talking to a friend; "Look, see that man? Wait! Turn your head away, look at me, keep talking. I wouldn't like it if he glanced this way and spotted me.... Can I tell you who he is? I can tell you, darling, it's no secret. That man was my husband."

In the second part of the novel we hear Peter talking to an old friend. "See the pair just leaving, there by the revolving doors? That woman there. The blond one in the round hat? No, the tall one in the mink, yes...They were sitting at that table in the corner earlier....That woman was my wife... We've been divorced for three years"

Judit, the third character and probably the most interesting, talks to her lover about her relation with Peter and Peter's family since she worked as a maid in their home starting when she was 15 years old.

Their different social and economic backgrounds are brilliantly exposed in these monologues and seems to be even more relevant than the romantic aspects of their relationships.

Ilonka explains what the differences are between her and Peter before they got married describing the problems of a middle class woman marrying a richer husband... "Everything was just a little different in their home compared with ours. We lived in a rented apartment; they in a rented villa. We had a balcony with geraniums; they had a little garden with two flower beds and an old walnut tree. We had an ordinary icebox that we filled with ice in summer while my mother-in-law had a small electric refrigerator"

On these same issue Peter tells his friend that he belongs to the middle class but "I was rich" he confesses and .. my wife's family was relatively poor. Not that being middle-class is a matter of money."

By stark contrast, Judit who, as peasant, deals with extreme poverty as a child becoming a servant and eventually marries Peter, crossing the class structure. As she proudly describes her family's background she said; "My father harvested melons ..... We were so poor we had to dig a shelter in the ditch and live there through winter, together with the field mice. But whenever I think of my father, you know, I picture him as a gentleman "

Portraits of a Marriage, as all Sándor Márai's books, is filled with details of its characters' feelings out of their vivid conversations. Márai is excelled at portraying time and place; emotions and situations. In this as in all his work, a profound understanding of the human conditions is revealed. This note with the quotes from the novel intends to serve as an "appetizer" to offer a taste of a complex and enjoyable story-telling.

Sándor Marai was born in Hungary in 1900 and emigrated to the US in 1948 to avoid Communism. Clearly he did not want to lose his freedom and individuality. He committed suicide in 1989. What led him to finish his own life is unknown and there are many interpretations. For example, Johanna Granville, a scholar from Wilson Center, reviewing Marai's Memoir of Hungary, 1944-48, think s that it was "a combination of the trauma of Soviet occupation and the identity crisis of a writer torn between East and West.."

Like many of his admirers, I am strongly convinced that he truly deserved the Nobel Prize for Literature taking into account the high quality of his works.

Excerpts From:

Sándor Márai, *Portraits of a Marriage* translated from the Hungarian by George Szirtes." Alfred A. Knopf, 2011 iBooks.

https://itunes.apple.com/us/book/portraits-of-a-marriage/id420425262?mt=11

Albert Camus, *The Fall*, Translated from the French by Justin O'Brien, Alfred A. Knopf, 1991. iBooks. https://itun.es/us/K4JkH.l

3. Sándor Márai. *Memoir of Hungary*, 1944-48. Trade paperback, Oxford University Press, USA, 1996

Joseph Conrad and the Darkness of Heart.

The Secret Agent.

Joseph Conrad is considered one of the most important writers in the 20th century. He was Born in 1857 in Berdichev, a region of Poland which today belongs to Ukraine. He became a British national at the age of 29, using English as his writing language.

Conrad is a prolific author who wrote dozens of short stories, novels, and travel journals. He excelled at the subject of adventures, including colonial undertakings in Africa. He is less known for his prophetical novels on the political intrigues and conflicts in Europe which reveal his profound knowledge and insight of these complicated issues.

Some situations portrayed in his political novels *Under the Western Eyes* and *The Secret Agent* could still be easily identified in the present time. Even if these extraordinary novels are fictional, both contain rich descriptions of certain terrorist plots or activities of the "agent provocateurs" and spies paid by foreign governments.

The main purpose of hiring these kind of agents is to warn their recruiting governments about the potentially dangerous activities of the radical groups. Governments that pay for this kind of "dark agents" also attempt to spread their influences in other countries.

The Secret Agent, written in 1907, is the story of Mr. Verloc, an agent employed by the French Government to report about the activities and plans of socialists, anarchists and other underground political figures living in London. These type of personalities would gather late in the evening in Mr. Verloc's small shop which, on the surface, sells "obscure newspapers, badly printed, with titles like 'The Torch','The Gong'—rousing titles" with windows displaying "photographs of more or less undressed dancing girls". Mr. Verloc was also one of the Vice-Presidents of an organization named "The Future of the Proletariat"

Despite all these links, Mr. Verloc enjoys a comfortable bourgeois double life with his family until he receives a "peremptory letter" summoning him to the French Embassy in the daytime, an unprecedented and unpleasant situation that can damage his image with his comrades.

He is received with some contempt by a new First Secretary, who says "I have here some of your reports" mocking Verloc's accounts as useless and expensive. "In the time of Baron Stott-Wartenheim (the previous French Ambassador) we had a lot of soft-headed people running this Embassy." And he continues, "What is required at present is not writing.. now we want facts…"

To convey what he means by "facts" and what Mr. Verloc is required to do to continue getting paid, the French diplomat explains that his government considers it "dangerous" that England has an absurd "sentimental regard for individual liberty position" opposing to tougher measures to combat political dissidents, soon to be discussed in an international meeting on security issues. "What we want is to administer a tonic to the Conference in Milan," he says, "..its deliberations upon international action for the suppression of political crime don't seem to get anywhere. England lags.", the bureaucrat claims.

The First Secretary carries on his monologue outlining his plan to "induce" England to accept new repressive policies. He orders Mr. Verloc to organise a series of terrorist acts to be "executed here in this country; not only planned here". That will shock and scare the middle class, turning them in favour of measures to make them feel secure. These acts, he says "... must be sufficiently startling—effective. Let them be directed against buildings...the fetish of the hour that all the bourgeoisie recognise...".

Almost as an anticipated ominous warning, 94 years after this novel was published, the U.S. suffered a series of well-planned terrorist attacks in 2001, mainly targeted at buildings, killing more that 3,000 people and destroying the Twin Towers of the World Trade Center, one of the most famous Manhatan landmarks.

In this classical novel, Joseph Conrad demonstrates his deep understanding of the radical minds of his time behind convulsive political intrigues that created tensions and serious conflicts, ending with the First World War.

It is clear that Conrad was aware of the destructive nature of radical ideologies that tended to justify violence and terrorism, disregarding innocent human lives for the sake of an abstract cause. In *The Secret Agent* and *Under the Western Eyes* he explores the so-called "Heart of Darkness", a metaphor of dark spirit, as used in the book title of one of his most famous novels.

These two works, written more than 100 years ago, are not

the only classic novels that deal with these current complex political and social topics. Dostoyevsky, some 30 years before Conrad, wrote *The Possessed*, a.k.a. Devils or Demons, which also tackles terrorism, a topic that regrettably continues to be very much alive today.

Excerpts From: Conrad, Joseph. "The Secret Agent." iBooks. https://itunes.apple.com/WebObjects/MZStore.woa/wa/viewBook?id=395547608

Joseph Conrad and the Darkness of Heart.
"Under the Western Eyes

Under the Western Eyes, first published in 1911, is the other remarkable novel written by Conrad dealing with the dark human aspects linked to extreme ideologies. Unfortunately this destructive power continues to be very much alive today.

In *The Secret Agent,* Conrad describes the "dark heart" of a bureaucrat in great detail. The First Secretary at the French Embassy in London is ready to destroy a landmark building and, if necessary, to kill innocent people in order to force the British to adopt repressive measures against their political dissidents.

In *Under the Western Eyes,* Conrad chooses a terrorist as another example of the "dark heart". Haldin, the main character of this extraordinary novel, is a young Russian student who proudly identifies himself as a "destructor", after killing the hated repressive official Mr. P— and possibly bystanders by throwing a bomb.

Following the successful terrorist act, Haldin hides in the home of Razumov, a lonely student whose acquaintance he made in university. He immediately feels that his future is threatened by Haldin's ominous presence in his quarters. Haldin says "It was I who removed P— this morning." trying to make his situation clear, and goes on in a challenging tone: "Men like me are necessary to make room for self-contained, thinking men like you", demeaning his colleague, who now becomes an unintentional accomplice. "All I want you to do is to help me to vanish". With these words Haldin starts to set the stage for a series of events which radically changed Razumov's life as revealed in his diary "...I, who love my country—who have nothing but that to love and put my faith in—am I to have my future, perhaps my usefulness, ruined by this sanguinary fanatic?"

From here the story unfolds a full range of unexpected developments, showing Conrad's unique talent as a storyteller with details of the ominous symptoms of the time in pre-revolution Russia. In the story, Conrad uses quotes from a journal that Razumov keeps after his encounter with the terrorist to demonstrate his internal conflicts, family background and the painful awakening path that connects him with extremists and revolutionaries as well as with rich powerful individuals in both Russia and the West.

The plot uses Razumov's internal tribulations stated in his diary and the interesting conversations taking place in Geneva about the brewing Russian revolution and the incapability of the western world to comprehend it. As this emigre in Geneva explains to her English professor, "You think it is a class conflict, or a conflict of interests, as social contests are with you in Europe. But it is not that at all. It is something quite different". The professor, who seems to be Conrad's own mouthpiece, replies to his Russian interlocutor "A violent revolution falls into the hands of narrow-minded fanatics and of tyrannical hypocrites at first." The professor goes further in his negative views on revolutions: "The scrupulous and the just, the noble, humane, and devoted natures; the unselfish and the intelligent may begin a movement—but it passes away from them. They are not the leaders of a revolution. They are its victims: the victims of disgust, of disenchantment—often of remorse." Clearly here Conrad anticipates with great lucidity the future of the Soviet Revolution five years later. Actually his comments are still valid taking a look at the negative results of the Orange revolution in Ukraine and the Spring revolutions in the Middle East.

Among other characters living in Geneva, Under the Western Eyes also includes an influential Russian writer who advocates radical feminists ideas, and Madame de S—, a rich lady with an aristocratic family background, famous for hosting "soirees" in her chateau with Russians and political conspirators. The character of Madame de S seems to have been inspired by Mme de Staël, the 19th century French political writer, who also lived near Geneva in a chateau and was famous for her "salon" style gatherings, attended by refugees and political thinkers in the Napoleonic era

This year is the 100th anniversary of the beginning of the World War I in which millions lost their lives. That war was triggered by the assassination of Austrian Archduke Franz Ferdinand and his wife in Sarajevo on June 28, 1914, three years after Under the Western Eyes was published.

There are remarkable resemblances between the fictional events of this novella and the actual occurrences which bring about historic implications. In Conrad's novel, Mr. P—, Haldin's target, survives during the terrorist attack while driven in a two-horse uncovered sleigh with a coachman who gets killed instead whereas in real life Archduke Franz Ferdinand was riding in an open-topped car when a terrorist threw two grenades that missed the royal member but wounded the officers badly in the car behind. In both cases, the assassination plot is completed by a second terrorist: in the novel, Haldin throws a bomb that kills the standstill target whereas in history, after the first failed attempt, Princip, the assassin, fired two shots to an almost motionless car killing the Archduke in Sarajevo and resulting in World War I.

These similarities that could be considered premonitions were again repeated 90 years later with the assassination of John F. Kennedy in Dallas, 1963. Moreover, terrorist acts that target buildings as in *The Secret Agent* mentioned in the previous chapter, turned into tragic reality on September 11, 2001 with the attacks on the Twin Towers in New York, igniting the wars in Iraq and Afghanistan.

Reading *Under the Western Eyes* and *The Secret Agent* certainly helps readers to better understand what Joseph Conrad meant by "Heart of Darkness" the title of one of his best well-known novels.

Excerpt From:

Joseph Conrad's *Under the Western Eyes*, 1911.

iBooks. https://itun.es/us/PSzUD.l

Letters as an Art Form and a Source of History
Part I: Thomas Mann-Herman Hesse

Books with collections of letters written by prominent artists, writers, thinkers, politicians, psychotherapists etc. are rich sources of knowledge which help us to understand different aspects of human nature such as love and friendship and others.

This literary genre allows readers to explore various facets of the personality and temperament of especially those who disguised they true nature or were distorted in their biographies which are sometimes full of lies and self flatteries.

Most of the published letters contain personal exchanges between people that dedicated time and passion to correspond with their lovers, families, friends and so forth. Such material reveals the personality, mood, taste, and personal challenges of the letter-writers. It also gives us the opportunity to get to know the atmosphere of their times and in some cases what was happening when the letters were written, including the spirit of their times, i.e. *Zeitgeist*.

In general, published correspondences were kept and organized by the writers and/or the addressees, and after their death, these writings passed on to their families or friends, which sometimes resulted in their ending up in museums or foundations or private collections. These institutions or individuals that are in possession of the collections sometimes license the rights to publish books with selections made by experts or authors' close relatives, who sometimes provide the context of the letters.

Letters also serve as an important source of information for biographers who can quote the writers directly expressing their own voices and intimate feelings that are always relevant for the readers to understand a writer's character. For example, the controversial Russian author Lou Andreas-Salome used letters to support the biographies on the life and works of Frederick Nietzsche and passionate poet Rainer Maria Rilke respectively, both were romantically linked to her in their lifetime.

There are also many examples of fictional letters that are regularly used in novels as part of a plot, including Ian McEwan's recent novel *Sweet Tooth* in which letters form an essential part of the story. Fictional letters are also used in *The Flash* and *Outbreak of a Fiery Mind* by Dale M. Moyer Ph.D. who published the imaginary correspondences that "Martha Bernays wrote to her fiancé, Sigmund Freud during the four years of their engagement." Irving Yalom in his novel *When Nietzsche Wept* used letters from this famous philosopher to build up a fictional story based on real life events.

We find multiple examples of films in which letters play a central role in the story. A good example is *The Go Between* (1970) by Joseph Losey where in the summer of 1900, a 13-year-old boy helped to carried letters between two secret lovers. The film is based on a novel by L.P. Hartley with the same tile.

Likewise, the form of letters is used in plays such as Vita and Virginia by Eileen Atkins, which is heavily based on the intelligent and passionate letters between the two British writers Vita Sackville-West and Virginia Woolf who exchanged letters for some 20 years until Woolf's suicide in 1941. Actresses Vanessa Redgrave and Eileen Atkins payed the two writers when the play was premiered in New York in 1994.

I would like to mention a few collections of letters, mainly from some letter-writers who lived between the end of the 19th century and the first half of the 20th century, a turbulent era with two devastating World Wars but at the same time full of creativity and romanticism.

I will provide some of the historic contexts and literary backgrounds, starting with the correspondences between Thomas Mann and Herman Hesse, the two renowned literature Nobel Prize winners, including texts that showed their fears during the rise of Nazism in Germany and the arrival of Hitler's arrival to power.

Letters as an Art Form and a Source of History. Part II.
Rilke, Kafka, Van Gogh, Freud, Churchill, Lennon

I will provide some of the historic contexts and literary backgrounds, starting with the correspondences between Thomas Mann and Herman Hesse, two renowned literature Nobel Prize winners, including texts that showed their fears during the rise of Nazism in Germany and Hitler's arrival to power. They wrote about the impact of this dark regime in their literary works as well as their feelings on witnessing the tragedy their own country was going through during those years. Even in the early days of Hitler both authors sensed that something very wrong was happening to their country. As Thomas Mann mentioned in his letter dated July 1933 to Hesse, "Day by day news from Germany, the deceit, the violence, the ridiculous show of 'historical grandeur', the sheer cruelty, fill me with horror, contempt and revulsion". In 1934 Mann wrote, "I am so plagued by the happenings in Germany, they are such a torment to my moral and critical conscience, that I seem to be unable to carry on with my current literary work." Hesse, on the other hand, expressed his fear for the safety of his family and close friends, "At the moment any wrath aroused by my name is likely to bring physical mistreatment and other troubles on my friends", he wrote in February 1937. By contrast, in most of their letters, there are direct references to the books which they were reading and what they were writing at that time. With great eloquence, Pete Hamill wrote an introduction to the latest

English re-print edition by Jorge Pinto Books, describing his experience reading the letters, "...I feel like some privileged guest in a special room, sitting off to the side somewhere, listening while these men talk."

To complement the views of these two exceptional writers regarding the horrors which followed Hitler's destructive path from the early 1930s, there are also some relevant passages in the letter that Winston Churchill wrote to his wife Clementine before the UK's involvement in World War II, giving his account of the events that had led to the war. These personal letters provide a spontaneous personal description of the challenges that his country and Europe were facing at the time.

In a less somber theme, I find Rainer Maria Rilke's letters to Lou Andreas-Salome refreshing, under the title *Rilke and Andreas-Salome: a love story in letters* and his own *Letters to a Young Poet*, which include references to poetry and love. The content of these letters show his frankness and desire for intellectual conversations and are full of wisdom, showing at the same time the unique passionate sensibility of this great artist and his immense capacity to express and discuss love.

The same characteristic can also be found in the letters of Franz Kafka to his two lovers, Milena and Felice, to whom he almost wrote daily. From the two collections, we realize that Kafka is not only a great novelist but also a fertile and passionate correspondent.

The collections of avant-garde artist Van Gogh's letters to Theo, his brother, are full of references to what art and painting meant to him as well as to other famous artists such as Monet and Gauguin.

The extensive correspondence of Sigmund Freud to his fiancé, colleagues, patients, friends and family members show how the Father of Psychoanalysis used letters to share his knowledge and insight of the human condition way beyond his professional realm.

Sending letters in the past required time and patience. Correspondence has its own protocol: once a letter is completed, it is usually sent folded in an envelope and, in some cases, sealed with wax to avoid tampering. Some rich individuals and government officials have their own trusted messengers; others might ask friends or relatives to deliver their letters just to feel more secure. Postal services have existed since ancient times in a relay fashion similar to ours, with one messenger passing letters on to another at a certain post or tavern along defined routes linking different cities and even countries. With the introduction of a more affordable national postal service together with a growing educated and well-traveled middle class in the mid-18th century, letter writing began to flourish with messages exchanged almost globally. That form of communication requires people to wait patiently for weeks before the postmen bring replies to their messages. To illustrate what expecting a letter meant I would like to quote from the final paragraph of one of Mrs. Churchill's letters to her husband Winston in 1915: "The post will be here in a few minutes & eagerly await a letter from you". Sigmund Freud seemed to be frustrated with the slow postal system and complained to Carl Jung in 1911, "I am writing you again this year, because I can't always wait for you to answer and prefer to write when I have time and am in the mood… ".

An interesting phenomenon of letter communication is the

fact that active writers, in general, are highly disciplined and tend to keep organized collections of their letters to make it easy for people to publish them after they die. In some cases, a close family member becomes the editor, as is the case with *The Personal Letters of the Churchills*, of whose selection and editing their daughter Mary Soames was in charge. Likewise, it was Freud's son Ernest L. who compiled and edited a selection of his father's letters addressed to Einstein, Thomas Mann, H. G. Wells, Maria Montessori, Carl Jung, Romain Rolland and many others, under the title The Letters of Sigmund Freud. Most of the editions of the collections of letters in the form of a book are made by scholars who are given access to the archives of the original copies.

Letters of famous people can be valuable tangible assets and kept in museums for safe storage and exhibition. For example, in the renowned Barnes Foundation in Philadelphia, the letters of Albert Barnes, its founder and collector, to various artists, intellectuals, gallery owners, etc. are displayed with detailed context and background to show how and why some of the art works of the Museum were acquired.

The material value of letters can be confirmed by the regular auctions where many important letters can fetch a big sum of money depending on who the writers are. To give an idea: the price of a hand-written letter from John Lennon to Eric Clapton reached a pre-sale estimate of US$20,000 to $30,000 in an auction by Profiles in History, a leading dealer in original historical autographs, letters and manuscripts. Two days ago the Financial Times published an article about a new sale of another manuscript by Lennon this time at at Sotheby's for the same estimated price.

Reading these collections gives a glimpse of the richness of the form of the written communication that is being lost little by little with the arrival of modern technology, including personal computers, internet and portable electronic devices such as iPhones and iPads together with many social platforms which have changed the way we read, interact and communicate with others.

The new media to communicate show a striking contrast through a simpler and instantaneous process: messages can be sent soon after finished with a click of a button. Particularly with improved eMail applications in smartphones, correspondences tend to be fast, made even on the road. Computers, smartphones and tablets have replaced ink, paper and typewriters, whereas internet and wireless communications have greatly diminished the role of the much slower traditional postal services.

Today, almost everybody is connected, receiving and sending dozens of emails a day and probably posting notes and photos on Twitter, Facebook and other social platforms or messaging services. The new communication styles are tremendously different from those of traditional letter-writing, reserved for private moments.

We can easily imagine that in the near future we will see books with selections of private relevant e-mails by famous people. Some of their e-mails could become valuable items for various reasons. Private disk drives and other storage devices could be worth a fortune. Just imagine the value of a selection of Steve Jobs personal e-mail archive!

The abandoning of physical letter-writing as a communication method replaced by electronic mailing is so unprecedented that Malcolm Jones, the well-known author of book reviews, considers that the "decline in letter writing constitutes a cultural shift so vast that in the future, historians may divide time not between B.C. and A.D. but between the eras when people wrote letters and when they did not"

Letters Part I & II. Excerpt From:

Hermann Hesse and Thomas Mann. Introduction by Pete Hamill. *The Hesse-Mann letters,1910-1955*. Jorge Pinto Books, 2006. http://www.pintobooks.com/ rediscoveredbooks2.html

Rainer Maria Rilke, Lou Andreas-Salome, Edward Snow (Translator) *Rilke and Andreas-Salome; a love story in letters* W.W. Norton, 1988 https://itunes.apple.com/us/ book/rilke-andreas-salome-love/id831234644?mt=11

Rainer Maria Rilke *Letters to a Young Poet.* Dover Publications, 2012. https://itunes.apple.com/us/book/ letters-to-a-young-poet/id504543167?mt=11

Franz Kafka, *Letters to Felice*, Knopf Doubleday Publishing Group, 1988. https://itunes.apple.com/us/book/letters-to-felice/id655193304?mt=11

Franz Kafka, *Letters to Milena*, Knopf Doubleday Publishing Group, 1990. https://itunes.apple.com/us/book/letters-to-milena/id655172328?mt=11

Vincent van Gogh, *The Letters: The Complete Illustrated and Annotated Edition*, edited by Leo Jansen, Hans Luijten, and Nienke Bakker, Thames & Hudson, London, 2009. http://www.frick.org/exhibitions/van_gogh/

theo#sthash.qtsHZYmd.dpuf

Mary Soames, Winston Churchill, Clementine Churchill. *The Personal Letters of the Churchills*.Houghton Mifflin Harcourt, 1999.

Sigmund Freud. *Letters of Sigmund Freud.* Edited by Ernest L. Freud. Dover, 1992

Malcolm Jones. *The Good Word*. Newsweek, January 17, 2009. Link: http://www.thedailybeast.com/newsweek/2009/01/17/the-good-word.html

Rainer Maria Rilke: *Letters to a Young Poet*, an astonishing wealth of ideas on love

Letters to a Young Poet by Rainer Maria Rilke is an outstanding collection of his correspondence with a 19-year-old cadet named Franz Xavier Kappus who aspires to be a poet but is struggling between a life path either as an artist or as an army officer. These beautifully written letters raise questions and apprehensions that Kappus and many other aspiring young poets shared in their correspondence with Rilke who was always modest to give advice and ideas how to deal with their emotional issues.

These letters are in some ways connected with Rilke's own painful experiences as a young man in his early years in a military school where he was mistreated and unhappy – a condition that led him to solitude and poetry writing. Most importantly, in the Letters, Rilke, at that time already a mature solitary writer, projected his own feelings and struggles to understand the difficulties of real love as well as the fundamental characteristics of human relationships, which he had been pursuing with great efforts.

Rilke's *Letters to a Young Poet*, together with *The Notebooks of Malte Laurids Brigge*, his brilliant autobiographical novel in the form of a diary during his stay in Paris, and the essays on August Rodin, to whom he became private secretary between 1902 and 1907, show his talent as an introspective prose writer. The content of these books blends naturally with his highly admired poetry books such as his beautiful *Sonnets to Orpheus*, the *Book of Hours*, the *Book of Images*,

Duino Ellegies etc.

It was Kappus who published ten letters that he received from Rilke between 1902 and 1908 and gave the title to the book in June 1929, three years after the Poet's death – we don't know how many letters he received as he only published ten. Kappus did not include his own letters in this volume. The readers would need to guess what he wrote to Rilke. In his brief Introduction to this book, Kappus explained that he had been troubled by his future as a military officer:"I felt to be directly opposed to my inclinations", therefore decided to send his "poetical efforts to Rainer Maria Rilke and ask for his opinion". Rilke answered from Paris, the beginning of a devoted correspondence between the two until 1908, "..then gradually trickled into nothing, since life drove me off into regions against which the poet's warm, delicate and touching solicitude had really tried to guard me', Kappus confessed in the introduction.

In his first letter Rilke talked about one of Kappus' poems. He suggested that he not show his work to anyone or send it to publishers so as to avoid rejection, "You are looking outwards, and of all things that is what you must now not do." "Nobody can help you", Rilke wrote, "Go inside yourself. Discover the motive that bids you write; examine...its roots down to the deepest places of your heart". Rilke showed in this paragraph a personal inclination for introspection, one of his own strengths as a solitary writer.

The correspondence shows that Rilke was often traveling since his letters were sent from Italy, Germany, Sweden and the last one from Paris. All his answers are full of wisdom related to the subjects that burdened Kappus in different moments and situations. He recommends him to read books starting with The Bible and J. P. Jacobsen's novels especially The Six Tales.

Rilke's letters reveal his generous personality by modestly sharing his knowledge about books, authors, virtue, sex, love, relationships, voicing his avant-garde opinions and ideas which even today can be considered controversial.

Like in most of his poetry, love and eroticism occupy a central place in the correspondence with Kappus who was at that time a young man experiencing romance and probably also physical contact with women. These letters allow Rilke to express his unconventional views on sex and love. He refers to the famous German poet Richard Dehmel, finding his poetry disappointing by turning "..what is charming into something unworthy". He goes further in his criticism by accusing Dahmel of being "no entirely mature" when he writes about sexuality in a way "which is not human enough, merely masculine, which is heat, intoxication and restlessness, and loaded with the old prejudices and arrogances with which men have disfigured and burdened love."

Continuing with the same topic in another reply, Rilke expresses his sympathy for Kappus' struggle to understand sex: "a complicated topic", he says, associated to many socially sanctioned ideas and misconceptions. "Our acceptance of it is not bad; what is bad is that almost all men misuse and squander this experience" Rilke wisely argues, probably recalling his own life.

The conversation on these topics is intensified in a letter sent from Rome in 1904 when Kappus seemed to have fallen in love. Trying to help the young cadet to deal with his natural romantic tribulations, Rilke expresses his views on what he considers to be real love, an emotional state that is very close to his poetry. With great candor and details Rilke writes: "..young people who are beginners in everything, cannot know love yet: they have to learn it", adding, they.."love falsely, that is simply surrendering, letting solitude go…"

Rilke frankly suggests to Kappus that he must be patient and let maturity lead him to appreciate love as a distinct "difficult" human experience that is different from mere sex, which according to the poet, the "..social perception has contrived to create shelters of every description, for as it was disposed to take love-life as a pleasure, it had to mould it into something easy, cheap, innocuous and safe, as public pleasures are". In the context of describing the difficulties of love, Rilke talks about what he considers to be a "good marriage", whose aim is not a "hasty communion…" but "..rather one in which each appoints the other as guardian of his solitude and shows him this greatest trust that he has to confer. "

The last published letter was sent from Paris in 1908, four years after the previous one in the book. In this particular letter, Rilke expresses the satisfaction of the fact that the young cadet chose the military profession of a "steady expressible existence" with title and uniform, "a duty, all this which is palpable and defined". Kappus served for 15 years as an officer in the Austro-Hungarian Army and continued to write poetry and novels although without too much success. Later he became an editor for various newspapers, including his own "Kappus Deutsche Wacht" and eventually died in 1966.

Rilke wrote more than 1,000 letters to friends, lovers, colleagues and some artists that he admired. After his death in 1926 his publisher acquired some and published most of them as collections which have been translated into dozens of languages. Among them, the most widely read are perhaps The Letters to a Young Poet, as well as those addressed to Lou Andreas Salom , a lover, a travelling companion and a long time friend. Letters on Cezanne published in English in 1985, is another important collection of Rilke's correspondence addressed to various friends about his admiration as well as the mystical experiences and influence that the famous French artist's paintings have on him and his poetry. "... after the master's death, I followed his traces everywhere", Rilke wrote in one of his letters to a friend.

We should be thankful to Franz Xavier Kappus for publishing Letters to a Young Poet, which offers an "astonishing wealth of ideas which the poet here raises", as Reginald Snell mentions in the introduction of his English translation of the book.

Excerpts From:

Rainer Maria Rilke. *Letters to a Young Poet*. Dover Publications. Print 2002. IBook 2012: https://itunes.apple.com/WebObjects/MZStore.woa/wa/viewBook?id=504543167

Excerpt From: Rainer Maria Rilke. *Letters on Cézanne*. North Point Edition: iBooks. https://itunes.apple.com/us/book/letters-on-cezanne/id498300676?mt=11

On Reading by Marcel Proust:

The Power of Books (Preface to John Ruskin's "Sesame and Lilies")

The taste for books seems to grow as intelligence grows. Marcel Proust

Books are not only powerful instruments to disseminate knowledge, but also agents of change. They are sources for joy and personal development as well as inspiration for freedom and democracy, to the extend that they even drive dictators to ban or destroy them. In order to understand better what reading books implies in Marcel Proust's preface to John Ruskin's *Sesame and Lilies,* I would like to offer first, as a context, some examples of books in the history of libraries and publishing.

The library has been a popular topic in numerous fiction books. For example, in *The Library of Babel* (La biblioteca de Babel), the famous short story by Argentinian writer Jorge Luis Borges, there exists a geometrical space or labyrinth with walls filled with books, including one with a magic and cabalistic content. On the other hand, in *Auto da Fé,* the novel written by Elias Canetti, a Literature Nobel Prize laureate, the main character has an obsessive and eventually tragic relationship with his enormous library. Among the non-fiction books dealing with the same motif, *The Library at Night* by Alberto Manguel, a renowned historian on books and reading, contains a serious study of famous libraries, from the biblical Babel and Alexandria to modern days, exploring the histories and anecdotes of book collections as well as their collectors, including a detailed description of his own library in France.

There are also many novels whose plots are based on either real or imaginary books. The famous novel *The Name of the Rose* by Umberto Eco begins with the following sentence: "On August 16, 1968, I was handed a book written by a certain Abbé Vallet, Le Manuscrit de Dom Adson de Melk, traduit en français d'après l'édition de Dom J. Mabillon (Aux Presses de l'Abbaye de la Source, Paris, 1842)." Here we have a complete reference of a specific book, including the date of publication. The story continues to tell the quest of "Le Manuscrit" while disclosing its secret content.

In this genre we can include publications with lists of favorite books by various authors and their recommendations. Over a hundred years ago a Russian publisher asked two thousand scholars, artists, and men of letters to name the books which were important to them. Tolstoy responded with a list with even the remarks of degrees of influence by ranking each title as: "enormous," "very great," or merely "great" (check below the link with the list of Tolstoy). There are also books dealing with the history of the most famous publishing houses like *The House of MacMillan* by British author Charles Morgan or At Random by Bennett Cerf, a writer and editor closely linked with Random House. These days some want to portray publishers as "villains", whereas these kind of books can help us to understand how the industry works and the important role it plays in promoting a culture.

However, the style of *On Reading* by Proust is so great and original, totally different from any conventions mentioned above, that I think it can be considered a "chef-d'œuvre". Proust used it as a preface to his own French translation of the English art critic John Ruskin's talk *Sesame and Lilies* published in the same book with five other of Ruskin's lectures that Proust also translated and annotated, i.e. Sesames of King's Treasures, Makeshift Memory, Ruskin in Venice, Servitude and Freedom and Resurrection.

Ruskin's presentation Sesame and Lilies was delivered in Rusholme Town Hall, Manchester, in December 1864. There, he told the audience: "..reading is precisely a conversation with men much wiser and more interesting than those we can know in person...reading, unlike conversation, consists for each of us in receiving the communication of another thought while remaining alone,..". It was published in 1865 and attracted wide attention at the time. It was considered a classic nineteenth-century controversial statement on the roles of men and women, but the main focus of the talk actually lies in the importance of books and the rewards of reading.

Proust never met Ruskin but Ruskin's works inspired Proust to write. Proust was also motivated to admire art, including a visit to Venice following the critic's steps. Proust took the task of making Ruskin's lectures available in French so seriously that he devoted eight years of apprenticeship to master English and eventually translate Ruskin's talks into French with his notes as well as an introduction to the lecture *Sesame and Lilies*. This translation in its entirety had been out of print since the early twentieth century until very recently.

Proust's Preface uses the same introspective style as that of his monumental work *A la recherche du temps perdu* (*Remembrance of Things Past* or *Things Remembered from the Past*). In *On Writing* Proust describes with great detail his experience as a young man on holidays in the countryside with his aunt and uncle, probably in Illiers-Combray. It is full of vivid illustrations of the mind such as the objects in his bedroom "these.. filled the room with a silent and multifarious life, with a mystery in which my own personality found itself at once lost and enchanted". He recalls the sounds of the conversations with the cook and other daily events of little importance such as his uncle brewing coffee or his aunt commenting on food, music or manners. I am especially impressed by the way in which he describes his irresistible urge to finish dinner or end outdoor games that he "was forced to play" as he could not wait to go back to his room to continue reading.

Proust also talks about the sadness that he feels when a book is finished, giving details of his desire to continue reading: he, like other passionate readers, ".. wanted the book to keep going, and, if that were not possible, wanted more information about all of its characters, wanted to learn something further about their lives,..". In another description of his feeling after reaching the end of a book, Proust notes "..when the last page had been read, the book was finished. With a deep sigh I had to halt the frantic racing of my eyes and of my voices, which had followed after my eyes without making a sound, stopping only to catch its breath."

Proust also dedicates some space to talk about the relationship between authors and their books, describing how "...the greatest writers, in the hours when they are not in direct communication with their thoughts, enjoy the company of books." then even adding "thinkers have a much greater capacity for productive reading (if one may put it this way) than creative writers". Another thing that Proust and Ruskin both strongly suggest is that reading should be an intimate activity practiced in solitude.

Proust reveals his philosophical wisdom distinguishing what historians and scholars seek by consulting books from what a regular reader expects. The former are looking for references to prove a theory or a superficial fact that they consider to be "a truth", in his own words: "...this truth that they seek at a distance, in a book, is properly speaking less the truth itself than a sign or a proof, something that therefore makes way for another truth that it suggests or verifies and this latter truth at least is an individual creation of his spirit." The latter, especially what Proust considers the "literary man" "reads for the sake of reading, to store up what he has read."

Proust here also shows his perception of issues related to psychological health as he writes about the healing quality that reading offers particularly to ease depression: "There are ... pathological circumstances one might say, of spiritual depression, in which reading can become a sort of curative discipline..." then, becoming more explicit, he adds, "Books then play for the person in these circumstances a role analogous to that played by psychotherapists".

In *On Reading* Proust lists names of many authors like Tacitus, Horace, Plato, Euripides, Ovid, Dante, Pascal, Montaigne, Diderot, Hugo, Molière, Descartes, Shakespeare and many more. But the only work that he describes with some details is *Captain Fracasse* by Théophile Gautier that he used to read in childhood, which shows the influence the book has on Proust.

We certainly live in a time very different from the early 20th Century when Proust translated Ruskin's dissertations and wrote the brilliant preface that we have just reviewed. Reading today can be conducted other than through books printed on paper. Technology allows us to bring our entire electronic library in a small device like an iPhone or iPad wherever we go. The supply of books has also become almost unlimited with the advent of "self publishing" which facilitates the publishing of one's writings. However, the challenge for us today might be how to dedicate time to reading and to getting quality reading material. It is very common today to find some people spend considerable time on emails and all forms of social media which many use obsessively. For those, we imagine, very little time could be left for real book reading.

In spite of the criticism and challenges that publishing houses face today, generally speaking, they are still the main source of quality books, with their professional text editing, type-setting and cover designs. Moreover, for centuries, some conscientious publishers have produced lots of "beautiful books", therefore, in Proust's expression, nourishing and promoting the most outstanding authors, including all the Literature Nobel Prize laureates among others. As Proust brilliantly describes one of his experiences finishing reading a book is like ending an intimate conversation with its author and its main characters: "... is one of the great and wondrous characteristics of beautiful books (and one which enables us to understand the simultaneously essential and limited role that reading can play in our spiritual life): that for the author they may be called Conclusions, but for the reader, Provocations. We can feel that our wisdom begins where the author's ends"

Excerpts From:

Proust, Marcel. *On Reading*. Published by Hesperus Press Limited, 2011. Available in iBooks. https://itunes.apple.com/us/book/on-reading/id482141696?mt=11

Umberto Eco. *The Name of the Rose*. iBooks. https://itun.es/us/IpbFz. Originally published Published by Harcourt, 1984

Jorge Luis Borges. *The Library of Babel*. In *Labyrinths: Selected Stories and Other Writings*, Published by Penguin Books Ltd, United Kingdom, 2000

Elias Canetti. *Auto Da Fe*, Published by Pan Books Ltd, 1978

Alberto Manguel. *The Library at Night*, Published by Yale University Press, 2008

Charles Morgan. *The House of Macmillan* (1843-1943), Published by Macmillan & Co. London, 1943

Bennett Cerf. *At Random: The Reminiscences of Bennett Cerf*, Published by Random House, 1977

Leo Tolstoy. *List of the 50+ Books That Influenced Him Most* (1891).

http://www.openculture.com/2014/07/leo-tolstoy-creates-a-list-of-the-50-books-that-influenced-him-most-1891.html

Albert Camus' *The Fall* and the First Person Perspective

May I, monsieur, offer my services without running the risk of intruding?

This is the opening of Albert Camus' novela *The Fall* as a vivid monologue in the "First Person" perspective, where the "I" and "you" used by a single person creates a dynamic and intriguing narration in fiction.

The main character, Jean-Baptiste Clamence, a judge residing in Amsterdam, tries to help a foreigner in a bar to order drinks while starting a conversation about the bartender's bad temper and the city. "Are you staying long in Amsterdam? A beautiful city, isn't it? Fascinated?" The dialogue continues but we, the readers, only can hear the narrator and imagine what the other unknown character replies.

"You're leaving already? Forgive me for having perhaps detained you. No, I beg you; I won't let you pay". A relationship has been established between two persons as the judge answers, "I shall certainly be here tomorrow, as I am every evening, and I shall be pleased to accept your invitation.

 The two characters will meet again and a conversation will continue with Clamence's voice revealing his background, his personal existential problems including a past experience that changed his life and makes him discover how empty and absurd his life was before.

 Other writers such as Sandor Marai and Walker Percy, they both distinctively adopt the "First Person" style in their novels

Portraits of a Marriage and Lancelot which are full of wonderful introspective dialogues and clearly reveal the main characters' internal emotions and their past.

Albert Camus, a 1957 Nobel Prize winner in literature, is one of the most influential French existentialist writers who have succeeded in applying the beauty of excellent literary skills on philosophy. An optimist but also a nostalgic solitary rebel, as the title of one of his most important essays *L'Homme révolté* suggests, he openly opposed the totalitarianism of what he described as "fallen revolutions" and "worn-out ideologies", i.e. Communism and Fascism, which inspired the destructive mass movements. He was not afraid to be isolated by opposing the popular ideas at that time, which led him to break with Sartre and other powerful intellectuals in the 50s that dominated the cultural scene in France. Unfortunately Camus died relatively young in a tragic car accident in 1960.

He sought solitude and the belief that a personal experience could be a persuasive reference for literary and philosophical writing which are reflected in his works especially notably in The Fall, a truly engaging novella which I think everybody should read.

Excerpts from:

Albert Camus. *The Fall.* Translated from the French by Justin O'Brien, Alfred A. Knopf, 1991. iBooks. https://itun.es/us/K4JkH.l

Sándor Márai. *Portraits of a Marriage.* translated from the Hungarian by George Szirtes." Alfred A. Knopf, 2011 iBooks. https://itunes.apple.com/us/book/portraits-of-a-marriage/id420425262?mt=11

Walker Percy. *Lancelot.* Open Road Media, 2011

Mario Vargas Llosa. *The Notebooks of Don Rigoberto*

The Use of Self-introspection, Diary, Reference and Conversation.

One of the greatest attributes of Mario Vargas Llosa's fiction writings is the complex characters which so well represent the diversity of Latin America's social and ethnic landscape. Using the voices of self-introspection, personal diaries and conversations, Vargas Llosa manages to create individuals with very different tastes, economic backgrounds and educational levels; women and men that are happy or sad; that love, hate or fear; that dream or despair.

With humor and satire, Vargas Llosa's stories deal with love, power, history and ideology, exploring a vast range of situations and problems that human relationships confront. Vargas Llosa's novels take the readers to Lima, Santo Domingo, Paris, Mexico, Buenos Aires and many other cities that he undoubtedly knows first hand.

His historic novels, *The War of the End of the World* (La guerra del fin del mundo) and *The Feast of the Goat* (La fiesta del chivo), demonstrate his talent as a storyteller as well as a serious scholar and journalist.

Most of his novels seem to be directly related to his own life. His second novel *The Time of the Hero* (La Ciudad de los Perros) tells about the life of certain young cadets who confront the severe hardships from the military hierarchy, which seems to be inspired by his own experience. His father sent him to the Leoncio Prado Military School in Lima Peru at age 16.

In a brief speech at the Nobel banquet in Sweden after receiving the 2010 Literature Prize,Vargas Llosa revealed his own background. He recalled the adventures of a 5-year-old boy – clearly himself – that read, discovering "a way to escape from the poor house, the poor country and the poor reality in which he lived, and to journey to wonderful, mesmerizing places peopled with the most beautiful beings and the most surprising things, where every day and every night brought a more intense, more thrilling more unusual form of bliss". He ended the speech by telling the audience that the protagonist of the story, now an adult, had received a mysterious call announcing "that he had won a prize and that in order to receive it he would have to travel to a place called Stockholm, the capital of a land called Sweden."

The Notebooks of Don Rigoberto, published in Spanish in 1997 was soon translated in English into 1998 by Edith Grossman. It can be classified as 'erotic picaresque", a genre that Vargas Llosa uses in many other novels. This one in particular is full of erotic content in the form of notes, letters and conversations that illustrate internal conflicts and delicious evocations of love scenes between Don Rigoberto, a highly educated man that is also an insurance executive and Doña Lucrecia, his second wife.

When the translation was published, The New York Times' critic Walter Kendrick presented Vargas Llosa's book as "a pornographic novel", focusing on the erotic descriptions in Rigoberto's mind and real scenes enacted by the couple in bed. Mr. Kendrick and other criticsmiss the complexity of

Vargas Llosa multi-layered narrative, which explores moral, emotional, physical and psychological issues, using images of famous paintings by Gustave Klimt, Félix Vallotton, Balthus and Fernando Botero, as well as quotes of Casanova, Marquis de Sade and many other classic authors skillfully chosen to be part of the story.

In addition to Don Rigoberto and Doña Lucrecia, there are two other relevant characters in the novel. One is Fonchito (nickname for Alfonso), the teenage son from Rigoberto's first marriage, who is so obsessed with Egon Schiele's life and his erotic paintings that he spends"hours looking at them in my papá's books". Fonchito also uses specific portraits by Schiele in "games" to try to seduce his stepmother "innocently" by asking her to "pose like the lady in 'Reclining Nude in Green Stockings...", while mischievously adding, "without undressing…" Lucrecia comments on Fonchito's actions: "The damn kid had the diabolical habit of turning the conversation to salacious topics, playing the innocent all the while"

The other character is Justiniana, Doña Lucrecia's trusted maid and confidant, who, despite of her limited education, has the sensibility to understand the complexity of her boss's relationship with Don Rigoberto and his son Fonchito. "She's more than an employee to me. I don't know what I would have done without her." Doña Lucrecia tells Fonchito, "I don't have the stupid prejudices against servants that other people in Lima have", referring to the thorny relationship that the upper classes have with their servants.

The story takes place in Lima and its three main characters belong to the educated upper middle class of the Peruvian society, which, as in most of Latin American countries, means that people with relative wealth can afford expensive homes, art collections, regular trips to Europe and New York as well as the luxury of having full time in-house staff like Justiniana. These people manage all the housework plus taking care of the children and, like in the novel, also of their boss.

.Don Rigoberto is a lonely individualistic executive full of mania and phobia kept in his notebooks, which are key part of the story. He reads and writes these notebooks late at night in his library revealing his sexually charged fantasiesand complicated relationships, many of which are inspired by books, paintings and music that he lists and describes with explicit details, which may be one of the reasons why some critics considered the novel to be borderline pornographic.

Don Rigoberto's life is full of contradictions. On the one hand, he "had already spent a quarter of a century at the insurance company, surrounded by, submerged in, asphyxiated by stupidity" and, on the other hand, is an erudite reader, peculiarly attracted to erotic art. As a collector he designs his library dogmatically to be "in the small constructed space that I will call my world and that will be ruled by my whims". He wants a library that holds "four thousand volumes and one hundred canvases and prints"and he adds,"to avoid excessive abundance and disorder, I will never own more". To explain his eccentric idea, Rigoberto writes, "... for each book I add to my library, I eliminate another, and each image that enters my collection— lithograph, woodcut, xylograph, drawing, engraving, mixed media, oil painting, watercolor, etcetera—displaces the least favorite among all the others."

Vargas Llosa offers an enjoyable multi-layered text, full of well-integrated references. The book is so rich that the readers are advised to make a list in their own notebooks of the books and artworks quoted by Vargas Llosa in this particular novel for the pleasure of further cross reading.

Excerpts From:

Mario Vargas Llosa. *The Notebooks of Don Rigoberto*, iBooks. https://itunes.apple.com/us/book/notebooks-don-rigoberto/id424009317?mt=11

Walker Percy's *Lancelot*:
a Philosophical Novel

Lancelot is probably the most controversial of the six novels written by Walker Percy, who is considered one of the greatest provocative "existentialist" voices in American literature. His first novel *The Moviegoer* won the 1962 National Book Award.

Percy followed the philosophical path of Jean Paul Sartre, Albert Camus, Søren Kierkegaard, Martin Heidegger and other relevant writers and philosophers. He was born in Alabama in 1916 and belongs to the extraordinary group of American Southern writers which includes William Faulkner, Tennessee Williams, Flannery O'Connor, Carson McCullers, William Styron, Harper Lee, Truman Capote, Tom Wolf, etc. Most of their works are marked by the "Southern Culture" which, for historical reasons, is different from the North and the West. New Orleans is one of the favorite places where some of the novels take place, as it is a multilingual city located in Louisiana, a State with a distinct culture breeding from a diverse ethnic population influenced by its background as a former French colony sold by Napoleon to the United States in 1812.

Walker Percy's life was full of tragedies. When Percy was 13 years old, his father committed suicide. Three years later, his mother was killed driving her car, which plunged into a river – many think it was intentional. He and his two brothers were then adopted by their uncle, a wealthy owner of a large plantation, a poet and a writer who was a friend of many important Southern writers including William Faulkner. His uncle, a lawyer graduated from Harvard, offered great help to the local poor and black people to get mortgage loans, which is noted by Peter Augustine Lawler in his anthology book titled A Political Companion to Walker Percy, the Percy family "..were vigorous opponents of bigotry and narrow-mindedness, especially when it was directed against Catholics, Jews, and Negroes". His uncle was also openly against the Ku Klux Klan, which was at that time very powerful in the South.

With the support of his uncle, young Percy attended the most prestigious schools. After graduating from Columbia Medical School, he worked as an intern at Bellevue Hospital in New York, where he contracted a rare kind of tuberculosis. He was then forced to be in isolation for three years at the Trudeau Sanatorium near Saranac Lake in up-state New York. Under the influence of his uncle's literary background, during this timePercy became a voracious reader of St. Thomas, St. Agustin, Tolstoy, Dostoevsky, Kierkegaard, Sartre, Camus and, for obvious reasons, Thomas Mann, whose Magic Mountain portrays people in a secluded situation similar to his. Due to this unexpected experience, Percy decided to abandon medicine and dedicated his life to writing, thus turning into a "confessed philosophical novelist preoccupied with the nature of the world and man's purpose..", according to Susan Lardner (Miscreants, The New Yorker, 02 May ,1997)

Percy's novels take place in New Orleans, where he lived most of his life, His main characters, like himself, are highly individualistic with a solitary nature and are inclined to explore their own existences, covering subjects such as social background, idiosyncratic traditions and religion, mainly

Catholicism as Percy became a Roman Catholic since marrying his wife.

Taking into account the number of suicides in Percy's family, the issue of "suicide" cannot but be present, implicitly or explicitly, in some of his novels. For example, in The Moviegoer one of the characters contemplates suicide and in The Last Gentleman a suicide actually takes place.

Percy's experiences with the recurring hurricanes in New Orleans, some with deadly effects, also become a motif of his novels. Furthermore, Percy tends to include the notion of "accident" or "incident" that dramatically changes the lives of the main characters in his stories and therefore brings them into such a depressed state that they blame the situation on what they view as the corrupted "Zeitgeist" i.e. the spirit of their time.

Percy incorporates all these elements as the key parts in the plot of his fourth novel Lancelot, published in 1977. The protagonist Lancelot seems to be locked somewhere like a jail or a mental hospital. The novel is basically an elaborate and complex monologue that Lancelot has with Percival, who can be a friend, a psychotherapist or a priest that visits him and listens to his story and troubled past. "...whether prison or not, is not a bad place to spend a year" he tells his attentive listener. By using the names of two of the most famous Knights of the Round Table involved in the quest for the Holy Grail, Percy seems to have drawn some parallels between the two stories. Lancelot, like the Knight, is associated with tragedy and adultery, ending up disillusioned in solitary confinement, seeking redemption after a series of calamities, whereas Percival is the Knight that represents the values of

Christianity. Another relevant reference is that in the novel Percy briefly mentions Queen Guinevere, King Arthur's wife who commits adultery with Lancelot.

In the beginning of the novel Lancelot tells Percival that he decided to kill his wife after he "discovered purely by chance that my wife had been, and probably was still, unfaithful to me". The "accidental revelation" conveys profound outrage and disappointment with life, a feeling that makes it impossible for him to have any form of trust in others, including romantic relationships. He blames the prevailing decadent culture of his time, sermonizing like a madman, "I can't tolerate this age.. Make love not war? I'll take war rather than what this age calls love. Which is a better world, this cocksucking cuntlapping assholelicking fornicating Happyland USA." Lancelot also associates his anger and resentment with religion when he says "God's secret design for man is that man's happiness lies for men in men practicing violence upon women and that woman's happiness lies in submitting to it."

In addition to the moral and religious remarks to justify the brutal act of killing his wife, Lancelot also mentions the political context of his indignation, telling Percival that his country "is down the drain. Everyone knows it. The people have lost it to the politicians, bureaucrats, drunk Congressmen, lying Presidents, White House preachers, C.I.A., F.B.I., Mafia, Pentagon, pornographers, muggers, buggers, bribers, bribe takers, rich crooked cowboys, sclerotic Southerners, rich crooked Yankees, dirty books, dirty movies, dirty plays, dirty talk shows, dirty soap operas, fags, lesbians, abortionists, Jesus shouters, anti-Jesus shouters, dying cities, dying schools, courses in how to fuck for schoolchildren." Clearly Percy does not share Lancelot's extreme opinions which, however, some people do embrace in the US till today.

Although Percy portraits Lancelot as a sophisticated thinker at times, in the end he looks like a deranged man so full of contradictions that he murders his wife without remorse. To make his character more complex, Percy adds the notion of "redemption" like the Knight of the Round Table. Lancelot tells Percival that once he is released from jail or the madhouse, he wants to marry the woman from the next door cell, who was gangraped and is recovering from the traumatic experience. Women must be saved from the whoredom they've chosen.", he explains.Lancelot wants to lead a revolution with his future wife to save the world from decadence, "we had both suffered the worst that could happen to us and come through, not merely survived but prevailed…we were qualified as the new Adam and Eve of the new world. If we couldn't invent a new world and a new dignity between man and woman, surely nobody could." he adds.

When the novel was released, it received some negative reviews, especially one from Christopher Lehmann-Haupt, a novelist, political activist and editor of The New York Times Book Review. With the title *Camelot Lost*, the reviewer considers that Lancelot's ideas are "downright upsetting. His treatment of an educated Negro as his family slave, his ridicule of the pretensions of modern art, his snobbery toward the socially inferior longing for acceptance and, most of all, his abhorrence of the liberated woman and his insistence that after his revolution "the New Woman will have perfect freedom. She will be free to be a lady or a whore", ideas that Walker Percy clearly didn't share. It seems that Mr. Lehmann-Haupt treats the book as a non-fiction, forgetting that the characters are fictional and also deranged. As a Southerner, Lancelot experiences with race might be different from a Northern liberal, but he is definitely not a racist as Mr. Lehmann-Haupt seems to have implied. The reviewer takes out the context of Lancelot's rants about blacks and women, showing bad faith by failing to mention that Percy was a socially concerned person and publicly criticizes any form of bigotry.

Written as a monologue in the "first person" p.o.v. enriched withphilosophical content, Lancelot is probably Percy's most difficult book to read. The main character and the only voice in the novel seems to be mentally ill. At times itinconsistently recounts the storyof his life in the context of a well-cultivated man who frequently quotes movies, classic existentialist writers and philosophers whomWalker Percy knew so well after years of studying their works. Percy is not only highly recognized as an extraordinary fiction writer but also asan existentialist philosopher who wrote several essays on Søren Kierkegaard, Martin Heidegger, Gabriel Marcel etc. Just a few months before Lancelot was released, Percy published The Man on the Train — an essay in which he explores some of the issues that Lancelot faces, particularly "alienation", a lonely existence lost in the crowd and psychological isolation in modern life, which he calls "everydayness". Lancelot deals with all these existentialist concepts; therefore,it can also be treated as a philosophical fiction.

Excerpts From:
Walker Percy, *Lancelot*, iBooks.

https://itun.es/us/u3SHz.l   Originally published by Farrar, Straus, 1977.

Patrick H. Samway, *Walker Percy: A Life*, University Press of Kentucky 410.

 Christopher Lehmann-Haupt. *Camelot Lost*, Books of the Times,The New York Times, February 17, 1977

 Walker Percy. *The Man on the Train: Three Existential Modes*. Partisan Review, no. 23 (Fall 1956). Hobson, p. 64. Later published in 1975 with other essays in Walker Percy *The Message in a Bottle* ,New York, Picador, 1978

Commemorating 100 Years of World War I Margaret McMillan & Joseph Roth regions.

Published to commemorates the 100th anniversary of the First World War that killed millions and devastated Europe. There are many books on the origins and the consequences, including a second more destructive war a few decades latter.

Among the most recent books is *The War that ended Peace* by Margaret McMillan, an historian of the University of Oxford. The title seems to dwell on the fact that "Europe had seen no major war for decades before 1914", only limited conflicts in Asia, Africa and distant regions.The first chapter has a vivid description of the Paris Exposition of 1900 that was visited by more than 50 million visitors. The French declared the Exhibition as "a symbol of harmony and peace".

The Introduction, as a stark contrast describe the destruction of Louvain in Belgium, once a "prosperous and peaceful" gothic town with a famous university founded in1425 with a library that hosted 200,000 unique books. In 1914 the town was destroyed and burned. The author mentions that "like much Belgium, Louvain has the misfortune to be on the route of the German invasion to France.."

The book brilliantly narrates the events that led to the war, the small conflicts and tension between that superpowers and their different allies through the aftermath of the assassination of Archduke Franz Ferdinand in Sarajevo on June 28, 1914, the spark that brought Europe to a war which ended the European empires and caused the worst chaos, death and misery to millions of people, including civilians, children and woman.

Among the fiction books that depict the human side of the beginning of a peaceful 20th Century and the horrible war, Joseph Roth offers two masterpieces, *The Radetzky March* (1932) and its sequel The Emperor's Tomb (1934). In the introduction of the first one, Nadine Gordimer mentions how Roth let us "see the deterioration of a society, an empire, in which disparate nationalities have been forced into political unity by an overriding authority and its symbol: the Austro-Hungarian Empire and the personality of Emperor Franz Joseph."

The Radetzky March is the story of a prominent family that was granted the highest ranks of the nobility for an heroic act of a soldier that saved the life of the young Emperor Franz Joseph in a battle. It described the life of the youngest member of the Trotta family and how the Empire was collapsing under the oldest emperor in the world. "All around him, Death was circling, circling and mowing". The huge power of the Hapsburgs was dying, "shattered on the ultimate bottom of the universe, splintering into several tiny solar balls that had to shine as independent stars on independent nations."

Some analysts see a parallel to the conflicts between China and Japan for some minor unimportant islands comparing these with what happened in the pre-war Europe 100 years ago.

I think it is a good timing to remember the First World War and its horrors reading Margaret McMillan's history book as well as Joseph Roth's brilliant novels.

Excerpt From:

Margaret McMillan. *The War that ended Peace.* Random

House, 2014. iBooks https://itunes.apple.com/us/book/the-war-that-ended-peace/id653545020?mt=11

Roth, Joseph. *The Radetzky March*. Overlook Press, 2002. iBooks.   https://itunes.apple.com/us/book/the-radetzky-march/id471195709?mt=11

Annex: Names of famous libraries, links and images.

The Abbey Library of Saint Gall, St. Gallen, Switzerland,

http://www.stibi.ch/en-us/info/openinghours.aspx

Bodleian Library, in Oxford, the United Kingdom,

http://www.bodleian.ox.ac.uk/hfl

The Vatican Library, Vatican City, Rome,

https://www.vatlib.it/home.php

The modern version of the Library of Alexandria, Alexandria, Egypt,

http://www.bibalex.gov.eg/en/default

El Escorial, Royal Library, San Lorenzo de El Escorial, Spain

http://el-escorial.com

Herzog August Library, Wolfenbüttel, Germany,

http://www.hab.de/en/home.html

Bibliothéque Nationale de France, Paris, France

http://www.bnf.fr/en/tools/a.welcome_to_the_bnf.html

Richelieu-Louvois Library

Austrian National Library Vienna, Austria,

https://www.onb.ac.at/en/

Biblioteca Palafoxiana, Puebla, Mexico

http://puebla.travel/en/see-do/places-of-interest/museum/item/
biblioteca-palafoxiana

Rijkmuseum Library, Amsterdam, The Netherlands

https://www.rijksmuseum.nl/en/research/reading-room

The Library of Congress Washington D.C.

https://loc.gov

Nakajima Library, iAkita, Japan

http://web.aiu.ac.jp/en/campuslife/nakajima-library/

Tianjin Binhai Library, nicknamed The Eye, Tianjin, China

https://www.mvrdv.nl/en/projects/tianjin-binhai-library

Note The selection and order of the list of libraries is random. To have a more complete list of world famous libraries check:

Jacques   Bosser   (Author),   Guillaume   de   Laubier (Photographer).The Most Beautiful Libraries in the World Hardcover, Harry N. Abrams, 2003

For those interested in looking at spaces and a list of libraries I suggest the following websites both with photographs of the http://www.thegentlemanscholar.com/Famous_Libraries.html (unfortunately without description of the content) and http:// mentalfloss.com/article/51788/62-worlds-most-beautiful- libraries (with a brief description of their collection, but with adds)

www.ingramcontent.com/pod-product-compliance
Lightning Source LLC
Chambersburg PA
CBHW020629130626
46552CB00003B/1149